the little book of
AFFIRMATIONS

First published in 2022 by Welbeck Publishing Group.

The right of Kate Delamere to be identified as the Author of the Work has been asserted by her in accordance with the Copyright, Designs and Patents Act 1988.

This edition published by OH
An Imprint of Headline Publishing Group Limited

Text and design © Carlton Books Limited 2022

4 6 8 10 9 7 5 3

Disclaimer:

Cataloguing in Publication Data is available from the British Library

ISBN 978-1-80069-177-3

Compiled and written by: Kate Delamere
Editorial: Victoria Denne
Designed and typeset in Joanna Sans Nova by: Andy Jones
Project manager: Russell Porter
Production: Rachel Burgess
Printed and bound in Dubai

MIX
Paper | Supporting
responsible forestry
FSC
www.fsc.org
FSC® C104740

Headline's policy is to use papers that are natural, renewable and recyclable products and made from wood grown in well-managed forests and other controlled sources. The logging and manufacturing processes are expected to conform to the environmental regulations of the country of origin.

HEADLINE PUBLISHING GROUP
An Hachette UK Company
Carmelite House, 50 Victoria Embankment, London EC4Y 0DZ

www.headline.co.uk   www.hachette.co.uk

the little book of
AFFIRMATIONS

kate delamere

CONTENTS

INTRODUCTION

One of the most positive people I know is my dad, whose favourite affirmation is 'Make the best of every day.' He taught me to always look for the positive in any situation for a happier life. And it turns out he was right! Research has shown that a positive mental attitude supported with affirmations will help you achieve success in anything.

Affirmations are special power thoughts to transform you for the better.

This *Little Book of Affirmations* is designed to be your best friend for whenever you need a helping hand of super power thoughts in your life, and is packed with some of the best uplifting quotes and positivity practices from influencers and celebrities.

You'll also find exclusive tips and techniques from experts such as positive thinker and famous spoon-bender Uri Geller, who discovered the benefits of using affirmations as a child, to international healer Sonja Grace and shaman Davina Mackail, both of whom use them in their work.

So, what are you waiting for? Today is a new day. Discover the power of affirmations and give birth to a new and better you!

CHAPTER

1

the POWER of AFFIRMATIONS

Affirmations are power thoughts –
positive phrases or statements
to challenge negative or unhelpful
thoughts.

They are thought
conditioners for positive
growth – and often
just a short, positive
statement, in the present
tense, said as a truth.

The word
affirmation
comes from
the Latin *affirmare*,
meaning
'to make steady,
strengthen'.

They can be used to empower every area of your life, from work, relationships and health to fostering self-belief, motivation and abundance in your life.

good reasons for doing them

Saying, hearing
or writing a positive
affirmation repetitively
embeds it into
your brain as a truth.

They help us train our
minds to think
nothing is impossible
as well as helping
to remove
negative thoughts.

According to Johns Hopkins University, there's a strong link between positivity and health.

Studies have found that a positive attitude improves outcomes and life satisfaction across a spectrum of conditions, including traumatic brain injury, stroke and brain tumours.

According to research from the National Science Foundation, around 80 per cent of our thoughts are negative.

And a total of 95 per cent of what we think is the same as the day before. We have between 12,000 to 50,000 thoughts a day, so that's as good a reason as any for trying to replace them with positive statements!

Affirmations are beneficial in improving negative thoughts because when you continuously make a positive statement such as,

'I am beautiful, and wonderful things are coming into my life,'

you are changing your internal dialogue. The more you make positive statements aloud and in your head, the more you believe them. Then your life becomes a reflection of those positive beliefs.

**scientific research
proves affirmations
work!**

Regular practice of affirmations has been proven to make long-lasting changes to the way you think and feel. By purifying your thoughts, you can literally restructure your brain.

MRI evidence suggests
specific neural pathways
are increased when
people practice
self-affirmation tasks.

According to Cascio et al., 2016.

A team led by Carnegie Mellon University's David Creswell found that people can boost their ability to solve problems under pressure by using self-affirmations.

Self-affirmations have also been shown to decrease health-deteriorating stress, replace negative self-messages with positive ones and stop us lingering on negative experiences.

Dr David Hamilton is a scientist and leading expert on mind–body interactions.

Writer and bestselling author of 11 books, columnist, public and corporate speaker and kindness scientist, his mission is to educate people on how they can harness their mind and emotions to improve their mental and physical health.

'After completing my PhD in organic chemistry, I worked in the pharmaceutical industry, developing drugs for cardiovascular disease and cancer. I was inspired by the placebo effect and how some people's conditions would improve because they believed a placebo was a real drug.'

As seen on drdavidhamilton.com

'We're also more likely to indulge in healthy behaviours and take positive steps to improve our lives.
This is especially the case when affirmations are repeated.'

Dr David Hamilton, *Why Woo Woo Works*

'They help us to think
and feel more positive and,
as a consequence, take
positive affirmative action.'

Dr David Hamilton, *Why Woo Woo Works*

CHAPTER

2

AFFIRMATIONS
and the
EXPERTS

ÉMILE COUÉ

Coué (1857–1926) was a nineteenth-century French psychologist who developed a popular method of self-improvement based on autosuggestions.

'*Every day
in every way
I'm getting better
and better.*'

Émile Coué

'If you persuade yourself that you
can do a certain thing, provided
this thing be possible, you will do it,
however difficult it may be.
If, on the contrary, you imagine
that you cannot do the simplest thing
in the world, it is impossible for
you to do it, and molehills become
for you unscalable mountains.'

Émile Coué

'If you are to succeed in anything, you must first be able to imagine it.'

Émile Coué

'The power of thought,
of idea, is
incommensurable,
is immeasurable.
The world is dominated
by thought.'

Émile Coué

'We possess within us a force of incalculable power, which if we direct it in a conscious and wise manner, gives us the mastery of ourselves and allows us not only to escape from physical and mental ills, but also to live in relative happiness.'

Émile Coué

NORMAN VINCENT PEALE

American minister Norman Vincent Peale
(1898-1993) is known as the father
of positive thinking. He is the author of
43 books including the bestseller *The
Power of Positive Thinking*.

Peale said that for a great day every day, it helps to think great thoughts and to concentrate on at least one every day.

As seen on guideposts.org

Create a weekly practice
by saying one of Norman's
affirmations on each day of
the week.

monday:

*'Love life
and it will love you
right back.'*

Norman Vincent Peale

tuesday:

'Change your thoughts, change your life.'

Norman Vincent Peale

wednesday:

'Change your thoughts and change your world.'

Norman Vincent Peale

thursday:

*'It's always
too early to quit.'*

Norman Vincent Peale

friday:

*'Keep thinking,
keep interested, keep
praying, keep
dreaming.'*

Norman Vincent Peale

saturday:

'The tests of life are not to break you but to make you.'

Norman Vincent Peale

sunday:

'Believe you can, and you can.'

Norman Vincent Peale

LOUISE HAY

Louise Hay (1926–2017) was an American
motivational author and one of the
founders of the self-help movement. She
wrote several self-help books, including
the 1984 *You Can Heal Your Life*.

She believed positive
affirmations
steer your thinking in a
healthier direction.

'Every thought you
think, every
word you say is an
affirmation.'

Louise Hay

As seen on louisehay.com

'Today I listen to
my feelings and I am
gentle with myself.
I know that all
of my feelings are my
friends.'

Louise Hay

As seen on louisehay.com

DR WAYNE DYER

Dr Wayne Dyer (1940–2015) was an
American self-help author and speaker
in self-development who wrote more
than 40 books, 21 of them bestsellers.
He is affectionately christened the 'father
of motivation' by his fans and was a big
believer in daily affirmations to help
manifest your deepest desires.

Empower yourself with Dr Dyer's
power thoughts:

'I am safe and I am loved.'

*'I am connected
to an unlimited source
of abundance.'*

'I forgive everyone,
including myself.'

'My essential nature
is perfect and faultless.'

'I nourish my mind,
body and soul.'

As seen on drwaynedyer.com

tip!

For the next five days,
get into a daily practice
of saying one of Dr Dyer's
affirmations out loud
after you wake up and
before you go to sleep.

AFFIRMATIONS OF FAMOUS PEOPLE

Many celebrities and influencers believe
affirmations helped them build self-belief
and play a big part in their success.

'It's the repetition of affirmations that leads to belief. And once that belief becomes a deep conviction, things begin to happen.'

Muhammad Ali
(1942–2016)

Boxer, activist and philanthropist

'We do not need magic to transform our world. We carry all the power we need inside ourselves already.'

J.K. Rowling

Author

*'Nothing
is impossible.
The word itself says
"I'm Possible".'*

Audrey Hepburn
(1929–1993)

Actress and humanitarian

In an interview with Oprah
Winfrey in 1997, Hollywood
actor Jim Carrey shared
how positive affirmations
helped him conquer adversity
when he was a penniless
actor and convinced him he
would one day make it.

As seen on riseupeight.org

Jennifer Lopez says her day isn't complete if she hasn't done 15 minutes of affirmations.

She believes that they bring her success, help her stay grounded as well as strong and positive.

As seen on thinkup.me

'I am whole. I am
good on my own. I love
myself. I love the Universe,
the Universe loves me.
I am youthful and timeless
at every age. I am enough.'

Jennifer Lopez

As seen on hola.com

'If I don't have
any shadow I am not
in the light.'

Lady Gaga

Singer-songwriter and actress, as seen
on kidadl.com

'No one can
tell you who you are
except for you.'

Serena Williams

Tennis player, as seen on stylecaster.com

'I feel beautiful.
I feel strong,
and I feel confident
in who I am.'

Demi Lovato

Singer-songwriter and actress, as seen
on azquotes.com

Actor, rapper and producer Will Smith
is a huge advocate of positive affirmations
and credits it as a big part of his success
and happiness.

One of his favourite quotes is by Chinese
philosopher Confucius:

*'He who says he can and
he who says he can't are
both usually right.'*

As seen on thehouseofroutine.com

'I am better than
I used to be. Better than
I was yesterday. But
hopefully not as good as
I'll be tomorrow.'

Marianne Williamson
(1942–2016)

Author, spiritual leader and political activist,
from her book *A Return to Love*

URI GELLER

Israeli-British mystifier, psychic and famous spoon-bender Uri Geller is a great believer in the limitless potential of our mind and discovered the power of affirmations as a child.

The following quotes are from an interview with me in October 2021:

'I'm a huge believer in the power of affirmations.

Stating something positive over and over again instills confidence and banishes doubt.'

'I make it my life mission to spread positivity.

I tell people – "Think positive! Be optimistic! Stay hopeful!"'

'We use so little of our minds. Most of it is an iceberg hidden beneath the surface, unused.

We call it the subconscious. It's the subcontinent of a vast treasure house waiting to be explored.'

'Our subconscious is always listening and soaking up experience like a sponge.

Talk to the submerged iceberg and tell it affirmations again and again and it will absorb the message and make it true.'

'I would hypnotize myself before I went to sleep. Run target words through my mind three times before I went to sleep to achieve a goal.'

Uri Geller explaining to Kate Delamere
how the power of positive affirmations helped
him as a child

One of Uri's
favourite affirmations
is:

'I can'

'Become a positive thinker. Believe in yourself and create a target goal.

And always think of success. Be an architect of your life.

If your mind can go there, so can your life.'

Uri's daily affirmation:

'I have health, happiness and peace of mind.'

Uri Geller, as told to Kate Delamere,
October 2021

Uri's affirmation tips:

'Don't sound desperate as you say them – sound confident. Repeat often every day. Affirmations are a gentle form of hypnosis. They work slowly and make you feel great.'

As seen on urigeller.com

How to turn your affirmation into
a super power thought, according
to Uri Geller:

Write down your
affirmation.

Word it clearly.

Repeat it out loud every
day, as many times
as you want.

Speak it out loud
and clearly – don't
mumble – so the world
can hear you.

Visualize it as if it has
happened.

tip!

Follow Uri's example
and choose an affirmation
to say three times in
your mind before you go
to sleep. Keep it up
for a week.

Uri's affirmations to foster
self-belief

'I am strong.'

'I am relaxed.'

'I am happy.'

'I love myself.'

'I'll wake up tomorrow feeling great.'

'I am focused.'

Uri's affirmations to boost
motivation
and attract
success

'There's no turning back.'

'I am a winner.'

*'I deserve to get what
I want.'*

'I deserve success.'

'I am an achiever.'

'I get things done.'

'I'll do it now!'

'I know what I want.'

'I never take no for an answer.'

'Winners never quit.'

'Excuses are for losers.'

'Everything is possible.'

Uri's affirmations for
students

'I will revise hard.'

*'I answered
the questions well.'*

'I will pass.'

CHAPTER

3

HEALTH and WELLBEING AFFIRMATIONS

SONJA GRACE

Award-winning author Sonja Grace is
an international mystic healer who uses
affirmations to help people suffering
from illness and disease.

Harness the power of her healing affirmations.

Choose one of Sonja's affirmations to heal your mind, body and spirit any time you need one.

Say it out loud. Repeat as often as you'd like.

AFFIRMATIONS OF A HEALTHY MIND

Our inner child is an aspect of ourselves, the free-spirited part of us that still feels and experiences the joy of life as a child.

The following quotes are from an interview with me in October 2021:

"reparenting" your inner child

Your inner child is what helped shape you into the person you are today. But, just as it carries the positive aspects of being a child, it also carries the hurtful moments of our past.

By retracing our past experiences, the positive aspects as well as the negative, we can discover some of the reasons behind our fears. By understanding them and seeing them for what they are, that's when healing can really begin.

When facing challenges in relationships
it is important to parent your wounded
inner child.

Assure him or her:

*'I am surrounded with love
and support, I am seen and
heard. I am safe.'*

To combat fear,
reassure your inner child.

*'I protect my inner child
and keep them safe.'*

When life feels overwhelming, release
the need to control outcomes by saying
the affirmation:

*'I am at peace within
myself and turn... NAME
YOUR CHALLENGE... over
to my higher power.'*

When facing heartbreak after the loss
of a loved one or loss of a relationship, let
go of pain by repeating a few times, out
loud, on a daily basis:

*'I am always connected
to the Source of life. I am
never abandoned. I am
safe.'*

Use this affirmation when battling dark
times to overturn negative thinking.

*'I'm valued, respected and
loved. My light shines
bright and illuminates the
darkness.'*

Repeat several times a day and feel
the truth of the statement in your body as
you say it.

To boost your self-esteem, affirm your
self-worth by saying out loud:

*'I am secure in myself
knowing I am always
connected to a higher
power, and aligned with
the light and truth in
my heart.'*

When stuck in a rut, let go of the past
by saying out loud:

*'I am free from the old
ideas that confine me,
I am filled with wonder
and ease.'*

The best way to clear karma is to forgive.

Feel it in your body as you say it. Identify the area you feel it in. Acknowledge it, then visualize letting it go.

'I forgive myself and others for any pain or wrongdoing I might have caused.'

AFFIRMATIONS OF A HEALTHY BODY

Positive statements empower health and wellbeing and are an important part of healing, according to Sonja.

The following quotes are from an interview with me in October 2021:

Affirmations must be felt in the
physical body. When it comes to healing
any dis-ease, say out loud:

*'My cells are clear and free
of dis-ease.'*

For extra power, visualize healthy cells
throughout your body boosting your
immune system.

It is vital to reset your mind and body
to release blocks that can create dis-ease.

Free yourself from identifying
with dis-ease and move forward, saying:

'I am free.'

When you say the affirmation, tap your
fingers on your thymus gland behind your
breastbone to stimulate it. This gland
produces white blood cells that play an
important part of body's immune system
which fights infection.

Earth yourself to attract more joy
into your life. Go outside and draw earth
energy up through your feet and legs
into your body.

Affirm:

*'I am one with the earth.
I am filled with joy as
I ground my energy'.*

Negativity can cause emotional and physical trauma in the body.

Affirmations are a great way to clear the darkness of despair.

Say:

'*I am the light that transforms the darkness.*'

Feel the light within you at the centre of your heart. Let it shine!

Dis-ease can be overturned with
forgiveness that needs to be felt inside
the body.

Forgive yourself for any past actions.
Imagine sitting in front of yourself and
looking deep into your eyes.
Then say out loud:

*'I love you. I forgive you.
Please forgive me.'*

Repeat this every day until the
feeling shifts.

AFFIRMATIONS FOR A HEALTHY SPIRIT

The following quotes are from an interview with me in October 2021:

'We come from divine
love and our job on earth
is to bring that into
physical form.'

'I am divine love.
I radiate kindness,
forgiveness and
compassion for myself
and others.
I choose the path of
the heart.'

When struggling to find peace of mind,
focus on the well of infinite peace in your
soul body in your heart and affirm:

*'I am at peace and my
soul body is aligned with
divine love.'*

Hope is key to survival on earth and to
remain connected to the Source of life.

*'I am filled with hope and
my future is bright, healthy,
prosperous and filled
with love.'*

The spiritual seeker desires enlightenment.
Along with a meditation practice, we must
do the inner emotional work to reach
higher states of consciousness.
Release the ego.

*'I surrender my attachment
to all things and release my
ego. I trust a higher power
to guide me.'*

CHAPTER

4

ENERGY
and VITALITY
AFFIRMATIONS

Dip into these affirmations
for a boost any time of the day
or night.

*'I'm letting go of the person
I was and becoming the
amazing woman/man I am.'*

*'Every day I step into the
best version of myself.'*

*'My imperfections and flaws
are where my beauty lies.'*

'I walk in my light and shine.'

'For me nothing is impossible.'

'I achieve anything I desire.'

'I let go of my worries
and fears.'

'I trust that all will be well.'

'Every day I love myself
that little bit more.'

'My mind is at peace and
my heart is full of joy.'

'I love and approve of
myself exactly as I am.'

'All my mistakes lead to
greater opportunities.'

'I recognize every
new challenge as an
opportunity.'

'All my actions are geared
to achieving my goals.'

'I spot opportunities and
act on them.'

'New doors are always opening for me.'

'I live in the now and plan for the future.'

'My success is a result of right thinking and hard work.'

DAVINA MACKAIL

Davina Mackail is a shaman and has spent many years practicing Peruvian shamanism. She makes regular TV appearances and has gained huge popularity as the *Dream Whisperer* on *The Wright Stuff*.

The following quotes are from an interview with me in October 2021:

Davina recommends using affirmations to boost energy levels, especially when you're feeling weighed down, uninventive or blocked.

'Our energy levels are
dependent on seven spinning
wheels of energy in our bodies
known as chakras. They run
along the spine and connect to
the physical organs.

The energy levels of our chakras
directly impacts our physical,
mental and emotional health.'

each energy centre has a base affirmation

consciousness is the crown chakra   'I am'

intuition is the third eye chakra   'I see'

speaking truth is the throat chakra   'I speak'

compassion is the heart chakra   'I love'

will is the solar plexus chakra   'I will'

creativity is the sacral chakra   'I desire'

survival is the base chakra   'I need'

to be MORE CONSCIOUS

Affirmation:

*'I am pure presence.
I reside in the awareness of the
eternal now. I am one with all
that is.'*

to HONE INTUITION

Affirmation:

*'My intuition always guides me.
I listen and act on that inner
knowing with trust. My life
unfolds in joyful alignment with
my highest purpose.'*

for AWARENESS to SPEAK YOUR TRUTH

Affirmation:

'My words create my reality. I hear and speak the truth. The truth sets me free. My words carry power, presence and love. I practice honesty with every utterance. I live in integrity. I am whole.'

to FOSTER COMPASSION

Affirmation:

'Today I rest in the softness of my heart. I expand and open my heart to allow compassion and co-operation to blossom. I forgive myself and others. Peace flows through me.'

to STRENGTHEN YOUR WILL

Affirmation:

'I am radiant.
My inner power is in direct
proportion to the healthy
relationships I build.
I achieve with grace and ease.'

to BOOST CREATIVITY

Affirmation:

*'I am abundant.
Prosperity flows through all
areas of my life. I allow my
creativity to flow through me.
I live a fulfilled, joyful, healthy
life. I play every day.'*

for SELF-RELIANCE

Affirmation:

*'I am safe. I am grounded.
I trust myself and life to support
me. I am grateful for my healthy
body. All my needs are met.'*

Davina's go-to affirmation when she needs a boost:

'Everything is working out perfectly because I'm lucky. I've always been lucky and every day, in every way, my luck gets better and better.'

Whenever I get overwhelmed, I pause, close my eyes and repeat this affirmation. It works!

AFFIRMATION MEDITATIONS

Meditation is an effective way to be more mindful of your thoughts.

Combined with affirmations, it is a powerful practice to change your thinking into a more positive mindset.

Affirmation meditation
is the practice
of positive thinking and
self-empowerment.

DAVIDJI

Davidji is a globally recognized
mind–body health and wellness expert,
mindful performance trainer and
meditation teacher.

David has taught millions of people
around the world to heal their hearts,
plant powerful intentions and
manifest their dream lives.

He believes gifting affirmations to
another is a sacred way to
transform lives.

As seen on davidji.com

Davidji's favourite Sacred Gifts are the
following three sentences:

'You're beautiful!'

'You're doing a great job!'

'I love you!'

From Davidji's book, *Sacred Powers:*
The Five Secrets to Awakening Transformation
(Hay House, December 2017)

Make an intention today
to gift your own
three affirmations to
someone who needs them,
whether in person, on the
phone, via e-mail, text,
or social media.

FEROZE DADA

Feroze Dada teaches meditation at
London's Sylvan Healing Sanctuary and
the author of *Children of the Revolution*
and *A Disciple*.

The following text and quotes are from an
interview with me in October 2021.

Feroze believes
affirmation meditations
are a powerful
way to start and end
each day.

Make time today to practice his daily affirmation meditation.

TIME: From 5 minutes.

1. Find a comfortable place to sit where you won't be disturbed.

2. Take a few deep breaths to relax.

3. Be aware of your breath as you breathe in and out.

4. Close your eyes and bring your awareness into your heart. Breathe in and out into your heart.

5. Every time your mind wishes to engage in a distracting thought, bring your focus back to your heart. Allow any thoughts to drift away like the clouds in the sky.

6. Silently express your deep gratitude for the privilege of experiencing this earthly life as a human being.

7. You will begin to experience a feeling of love and compassion. Embrace this sensation as it fills you up.

Affirmation

8. Now recite this affirmation out loud three times:

'I accept with humility whatever comes my way. I surrender to each and every experience.'

9. Scan your body from head to toe and acknowledge any sensations without attachment.

10. Bring your awareness to your breath, then back to the room.

CHAPTER

5

GRATITUDE

This chapter focuses on how gratitude
fosters calm, balance and serenity
when feeling negative, critical, anxious,
hyperactive or nervous.

Gratitude is
associated with
feelings of
happiness and is
the antidote
to fear.

There are many health benefits to gratitude.

'Inflammation in one's body can decrease. Expressing gratitude reduces stress, increases optimism and changes your brain.'

As seen on positivepsychology.com

A 2018 study by the Greater Good Science Center found gratitude fosters better physical health, better sleep, less fatigue, lower levels of cellular inflammation, greater resiliency and encourages the development of patience, humility and wisdom.

When you are grateful, fear disappears and abundance appears.

did you know?

Abundance comes from
gratitude for what we have.

So give thanks to manifest
what you need.

Say out loud:

*'I am grateful for
all that I have and give
thanks for my life.'*

Affirmations to give thanks.

'THANK YOU!'

'I am blessed.'

'I give thanks for my
safe, peaceful and secure
home where I can
recharge and relax.'

'I am grateful for the love
and support of my family
and friends.'

'I am grateful for the
fulfilling life I'm living.'

'I am grateful to my healthy body for carrying me through each day.'

'I give thanks for a healthy mind and a healthy body.'

'The more I appreciate the
more I get back.'

'I am grateful for what I
have and excited for what's
to come.'

Write your own gratitude affirmations:

'I am grateful/thankful/ appreciate...'

Fill in the gap with what/who you are grateful to/for:

_____

_____

_____

_____

Say it three times out
loud in the mirror
for the most powerful
effect.

Say it whenever you feel
ingratitude.

CHAPTER

6

CREATING
your own
AFFIRMATIONS

Affirmations are a mixture of a mission statement, a belief statement, and a commitment statement.

When set up correctly, they are motivational and act to refocus you when you drift off course.

there are 4 rules to creating affirmations

1. Set a direction rather than a goal.

2. Make it a learning direction rather than a performance direction.

3. Make it motivational and exciting.

4. Amplify something you already believe.

WRITE YOUR OWN AFFIRMATIONS

step 1: keep it simple

**step 2:
keep it in the present tense**

Start with the words 'I am'.

The present gives your subconscious mind a command. Your mind interprets it as an action to follow through on.

step 3: visualize

Speak about things as if you already have them in the present tense. It helps your mind to visualize the outcome.

For example, 'I have a beautiful beach house flooded with sunlight' instead of 'This year I am going to buy a beach house'.

step 4: don't use negatives

Your subconscious mind does not recognize negatives.

So if you say, 'Don't shut yourself off to new opportunities', all your mind hears is 'Shut yourself off...' Instead, say: 'I am open to new opportunities'.

step 5: keep it brief.

Write something that's short and snappy.

Think 'I naturally choose healthy foods', rather than 'I always choose healthy foods over junk food because I'm mindful of my health'.

step 6: be specific.

Including a specific makes it easier for your mind to visualize the outcome. So, instead of saying, 'I will increase my income this year', say, 'I am enjoying my £100,000 earnings this year'.

step 7: write it for *you*!

Make sure your affirmations
describe your actions and not the
actions of others.

remember!

Whether negative or positive, affirmations work! Embrace the positive and avoid the negative.

Write them down and put them somewhere you'll see regularly, like your fridge or bathroom mirror, to remain focused on them!

tip!

To super-charge your affirmations,
SAY the affirmation, SEE the affirmation
and BE the affirmation.

As you repeat it, see yourself doing
it and relax into the feeling of having
already achieved it.

say it, see it,
be it

extra tips!

Simply make a start.

Take small steps. Saying one affirmation
a day is a good start.

Be consistent.

Repeat your chosen affirmation
every day. An action becomes a habit
when it is done regularly.

believe

Know you are worthy of what you desire.
Keep self-doubt at bay.

take action

Recognize opportunities and take
necessary action when the right people
and situations show up.

be creative!

MAKE IT REAL

1. The more real we make our affirmations, the easier it is for our minds to embrace how true they are. Imagine a natural image that compliments the statements you're making.

   For example, when writing an abundance affirmation, see an abundance of stars in the sky.

imagine the outcome

Imagine it using all your senses.

What would this reality look like?

Taste like?

Sound like?

Smell like?

Feel like?

This is an easy way to get your
feelings engaged with your affirmations.

As you imagine, your feelings
will create energy to bring about this
new reality.

WRITE AN AFFIRMATION LETTER

2. Sometimes you may find that your
   mind wanders when you try to focus
   on a goal in your mind. Writing an
   affirmation letter can generate the
   focus and details needed to create
   your new reality.

write a letter to the universe

- Write down your ideal day from sunrise to sunset.

- Write a letter to someone you admire about the qualities they have that you want to incorporate into your life.

BE IMAGINATIVE

3. Putting your affirmations into a picture or other work of art can be a great way to add energy to your affirmations.

- Paint or draw your ideal life or a symbol for your ideal life.

- Create a vision board or book.

SMILE

4. Smiling while you are saying affirmations fosters positive feelings. You will be amazed at what a great mood you'll be in when you start smiling.

FEEL THE ENERGY WITHIN

5. The energy that creates our desires moves within us. This energy is powerful enough to power our body and to change any circumstance we so desire.

   Tap into that energy by focusing on a part of your body and sense the vibrations in it. For example, your hands.

Before you say your affirmations, take a
minute to feel that energy in your palms
and fingers – perhaps it is a tingling
sensation – and remind yourself that there
is this power within you that can in turn
power your words.

TAKE A WEEK

6. Before or during your affirmations,
   walking in nature can be an inspiring
   act. Notice the colours, shapes of trees
   and flowers.

Take the time to notice the precision and creativity in nature. Know that the force that guides each tree and flower while it is growing is the same force that's guiding your life.

LISTEN TO MUSIC

7. Music is a surefire way to get your emotions roused toward your intentions. Say your affirmations before or during a piece of music and then let the music carry your feelings into your new reality.

Music also gives your mind something to focus on rather than wander.

Sink into the melody, and with your eyes closed, let the music become the soundtrack to your new life.

MEDITATE

8. Meditating gives your mind a break from distracting thoughts and can help you get in touch with the more intuitive part of yourself.

Meditate before saying
your affirmations to empty
your mind of distracting
thoughts so that the
affirmation can get through
to your subconscious mind
and plant the new belief
more effectively.

MEDITATION PRACTICES

Counting – count up, count down, count 1 to 10, count at each inhalation and each exhalation.

Meditate on a word – such as: peace, love, abundance, prosperity, joy.

Watch your body – focus on your breath moving in and out of your nose and mouth.

Meditate on your specific affirmation – repeat it over and over again.

Focus on an object – for example, the tip of a candle flame.

Use a guided meditation – led by a teacher, either in person or via audio or video.

tip!

If your mind wanders,
don't worry!

Just observe your monkey
mind jumping around and
slowly guide it back to your
focus point.

DID YOU KNOW?

Louise Hay recommended saying affirmations into a mirror for greater effect. She believed the mirror reflects back the feelings you have about yourself and makes you aware where you're resistant and where you're open.

It shows you what thoughts you need to change for a joyous, fulfilling life.

action plan

Take up a 21-day mirror affirmation challenge. Each day look into your eyes in a mirror and say an affirmation.

Then, after you've said it, thank yourself for your positive action towards a better you.

Keep a daily journal to
record any positive changes
in your life.
good luck!

CONCLUSION

I hope these tips and techniques have given you guidance and strength to instigate physical, mental or spiritual change.

Keep this book close for whenever you need to identify future trouble-spots, reframe negativity or challenges and refocus your mindset. Use the affirmations when you feel at a crossroads, are unable to move ahead or want to make change but don't know how.

Your mind is full of magical possibilities. The first step to tapping into them is to believe in yourself.

Make a commitment to put aside just a few minutes every day to put positive affirmations into practice.

They'll continue to transform your life, alter your mindset and change every area of your life for the better. The tools to transform your life are now in your hands.

So be consistent and, like my dad says, 'Make the best of every day!'

Kate Delamere
November 2021

'I have all
the strength and
confidence
within me
that I need to
succeed.'